YOU CAN WRITE A STORY

STEP BY STEP STORY WRITING FOR KIDS

First published in 2023 in Great Britain by
Far Lands Press
©Jackie Daw

The moral right of Jackie Daw to be identified as the author of this work has been asserted in accordance with the Copyright, Designs and Patents Act 1988

All rights reserved. No part of this publication may be reproduced in whole or in any part in any form whatsoever without the written permission of the author.

ISBN: 978-1-7396017-6-8

This Book Belongs to:

Every story has the same basic elements

Characters!

A Setting!!

A Plot!!

(This is where the action happens)

It's your story. You are the writer. Use your imagination to create the characters, design the setting and build the plot.

So let's get started!

It's time to meet your team...

Step One:

Characters

Choose Your Main Character

Whose story are you going to tell?

Is it your story?

Or maybe you can come up with a creation from your imagination...

 A magical octopus perhaps

Or a singing robot...

There are no rules! You're the story writer, you can create whoever or whatever you want.

CHARACTERISTICS

Let's make up some details about your main character...

What is their name?

What do they look like?

What are they good at?

What are they not good at?

What do they like?

What do they dislike?

What's their personality like?

What makes them special?

Draw a picture of your main character

There are some very important questions to ask your character...

Question 1: What do they want?

Question 2: Why do they want it?

They could want anything at all:

To be rich

To be famous

To win the match

But why?

So they can buy nice new clothes?

So they can show off?

So they can be the best?

Think carefully, as your story will be based on your character's quest to reach their dream.

Write down what your character wants and why they want it...

The Sidekick

Most great characters have a friend, a sidekick to help them on their quest. Some have more than one!

Sidekicks not only help the main character, but they also help you, as the writer, explain the story to reader.

The sidekick doesn't always understand what's going on- so the main character can explain it to them (and your reader).

Sidekicks can listen to the the main character's thoughts and tell them if they are making a mistake.

The Sidekick

Let's make up some details about the sidekick...

What is their name?

What do they look like?

What are they good at?

What are they not good at?

What do they like?

What do they dislike?

What's their personality like?

What makes them special?

Draw a picture of your Sidekick

The Villain

A good story has a villain, a bad guy. Someone who is trying to stop your main character from reaching their goal.

Villains are not always people or creatures- they could be:

a business- who want to destroy a forest

an emotion- like fear

or a physical obstruction- like a vast ocean or a towering mountain

Anything or anyone who is trying to prevent your character from reaching their goal, is a villain.

The Villain

Let's make up some details about the villain...

What is their name?

What do they look like?

What are they good at?

What are they not good at?

What do they like?

What do they dislike?

What's their personality like?

What makes them special?

DRAW A PICTURE OF YOUR VILLAIN

Write down what your villain wants and why they want it...

Character Suggestions

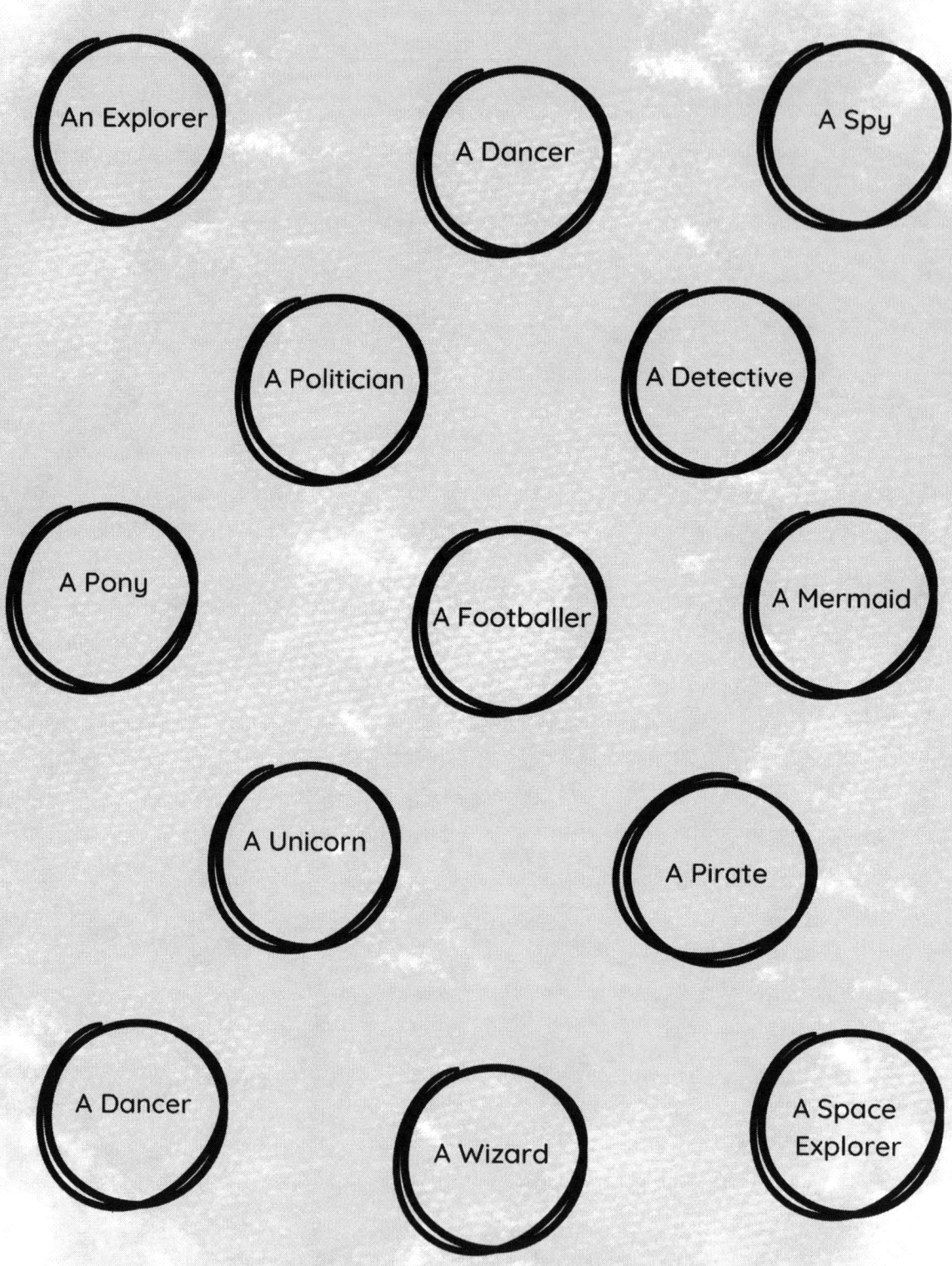

Re-Cap

So now you have your:

    Main character

    Your sidekick

    and

    Your villain

You know:

What your character wants

Why they want it

Who is helping them

and

Who or what is standing in their way

Now we need to decide WHO is telling the story...

Step Two:

Point of View

Who is telling the story?

There are several ways of telling your story but the most common are:

First Person

and

Third Person

First person stories are told directly by the main character.

Third person stories are told by another person about the character.
(Perhaps a narrator or you, the storyteller.)

Let's decide which is best for your story...

First Person

First person stories are told directly by the main character. Imagine the character is sitting in front of you, telling you their story.

They would say ... I

I went to the park and I saw a dog.

The good thing about telling a story in the first person, is that the character can tell you what they are thinking and how they are feeling.

The downside of choosing to tell your story in the first person, is that you can only tell the parts of the story that your character knows about and sees for themselves.

Let's try it out...

First Person

Write a diary entry for your chracter in the first person..

(Remember to use 'I')

Third Person

Third person stories are told by another person, about the character.

Let's say your character is called Bob.

The storyteller (that's you!) would use his name...

Bob went to the park and he saw a dog.

The good thing about telling a story in the third person, is that you can switch between the experiences of your main character, your sidekick or even the villain.

Let's give it a go...

Third Person

Write a report of a day in the life of your character in the third person..
(Remember to use their name.)

Re-Cap

So now you have your:

Main character

Your sidekick

and

Your villain

You know:

What your character wants

Why they want it

Who is helping them

Who or what is standing in their way

and

Who is telling the story

Now you need to decide where your story takes place...

Step Three:

Setting

Choose your story setting

To bring your story to life, you need to create world for your characters to live in.

Remember, this is your story, so you can creat any world you want.

Maybe your characters are:

From your own world, live in your house and go to your school

Maybe they:

Live on top of a mountain

On a boat

In outer space

Maybe your character:

Lives in the past

In the future

On another planet

The only limit to where you set your story- is your imagination!

Let's build your character's world.

Let's make up some details about your character's world ...

Where does your character live?

What does the world look like?

When is your story set?

What makes this world different?

Who else lives in their world?

What dangers are there?

Draw a Picture of Your Character's World

The Setting

Imagine you are selling your character's home. Write a description for the advertisement...

Setting Ideas

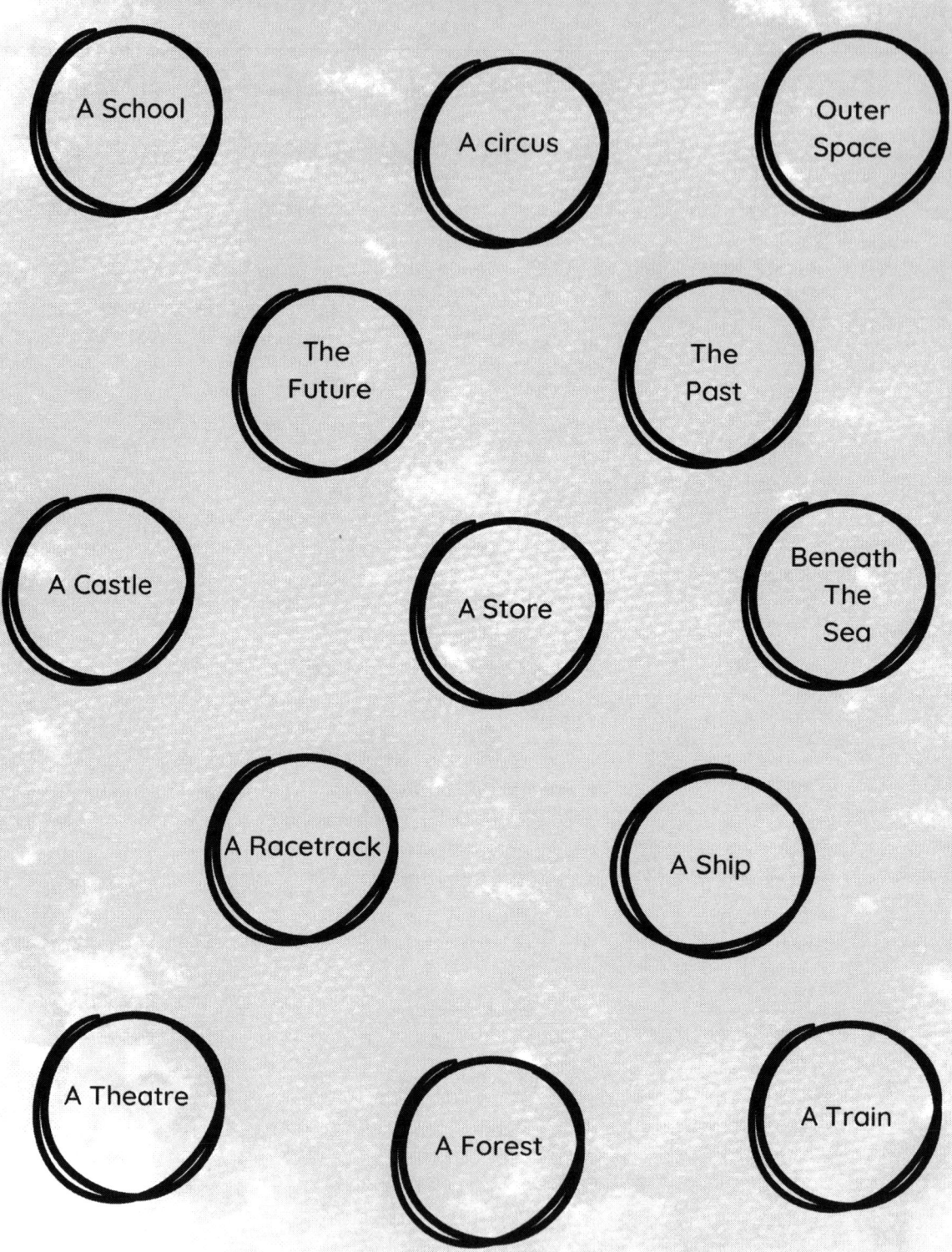

Re-Cap

So now you have your:

Main character
Your sidekick
and
Your villain

You know:

What your character wants
Why they want it
Who is helping them
Who or what is standing in their way
Who is telling the story
and
Where it is set

Now for the exciting part. Let's take your characters on an adventure in the plot...

Step Four:

The Plot

Write a Storyboard Summary for Your Story

1. This is a story about…	2. Who lives in…
3. When…	4. So…
5. But…	6. However…
7. In the end…	8. Reflection

Re-Cap

So now you have your:

Main character
Your sidekick
and
Your villain

You know:

What your character wants
Why they want it
Who is helping them
Who or what is standing in their way
Who is telling the story
Where it is set
plus
Your story's plot

It's almost time to get writing. But first, here are some writing tips to help your story come to life...

Step Five:

Writing Tips

Writing Tips

Descriptions

When you are writing description, close your eyes and imagine you are in the story with your character:

What can you see?

Hear? Smell? Touch?

How does it make you feel?

Use similes to liven up your descriptions.

A boy with wet hair could:

'Look like a newly hatched chick...'

Think of more interesting words to spice up your story.

Instead of:

'She loved cake.' You could say: 'She adored cake.'

Instead of:

'He ran home.' You could say could say: 'He hurried home.'

Take your time. Think about every word you choose. Can you find a better option?

Writing Tips

Dialogue

Adding dialogue (when your characters speak) is a great way of making your story more interesting. But you should try to vary the way you identify who is talking. If you write: 'he said' or 'she said' every time someone speaks, it can become repetitive and boring.

Think of other words like, he...

...replied

...answered

...muttered

...called

Another way to identify who is talking is to have them do something, like...
George shook his head, "No I didn't."
This way your reader knows it was George who spoke, but you didn't write: 'George said.'

Writing Tips

Pacing

The pacing of your story is the flow of the way the writing sounds.

You can write exciting action by using short sentences:

'He ran fast. He had no time. The clock was ticking down.'

But a whole story full of short sentences will sound rushed. On the other hand, very long sentences can take a long time to read and slow the reader down making the story seem boring.

If you vary the length of your sentences, depending on what is happening in the story, you should keep your readers turning the page.

Read your story out loud to see if it flows well.

Re-Cap
So now you have your:

Main character
Your didekick
and
Your villain

You know:

What your character wants
Why they want it
Who is helping them
Who or what is standing in their way
Who is telling the story
Where it is set
Your story's plot
and
You've practiced your skills

There's only one thing left to do!
Let's get writing!!

...

Step Six:

Let's Write

STORY ONE

Let's get started!

On the next page-
draw the cover for your story.

Remember to add the title and the author's name. (That's you!)

PLOT MAP

① This is a story about...
(meet the characters)

Top Tip
Start your story with action.

PLOT MAP

② Who live in... (Show the characters in their world)

Top Tip
Include smells and sounds.

Plot Map

③ When... (Something happens to change things)

Top Tip
This should change everything.

PLOT MAP

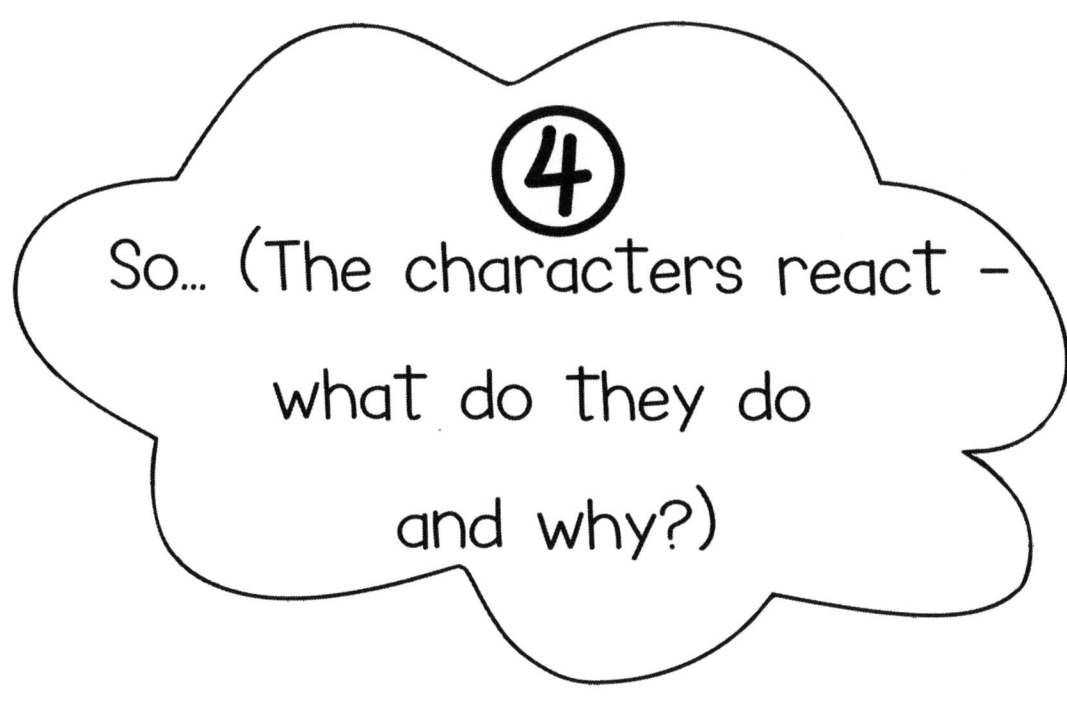

④ So... (The characters react – what do they do and why?)

Top Tip
Get them out of their comfort zone!

Plot Map

⑤

But...! (Something goes wrong)

Top Tip
All is hopeless...
or is it?

Plot Map

⑥ However...

(Your character tries to solve the problem)

Top Tip
Your character's special difference could help here.

Plot Map

PLOT MAP

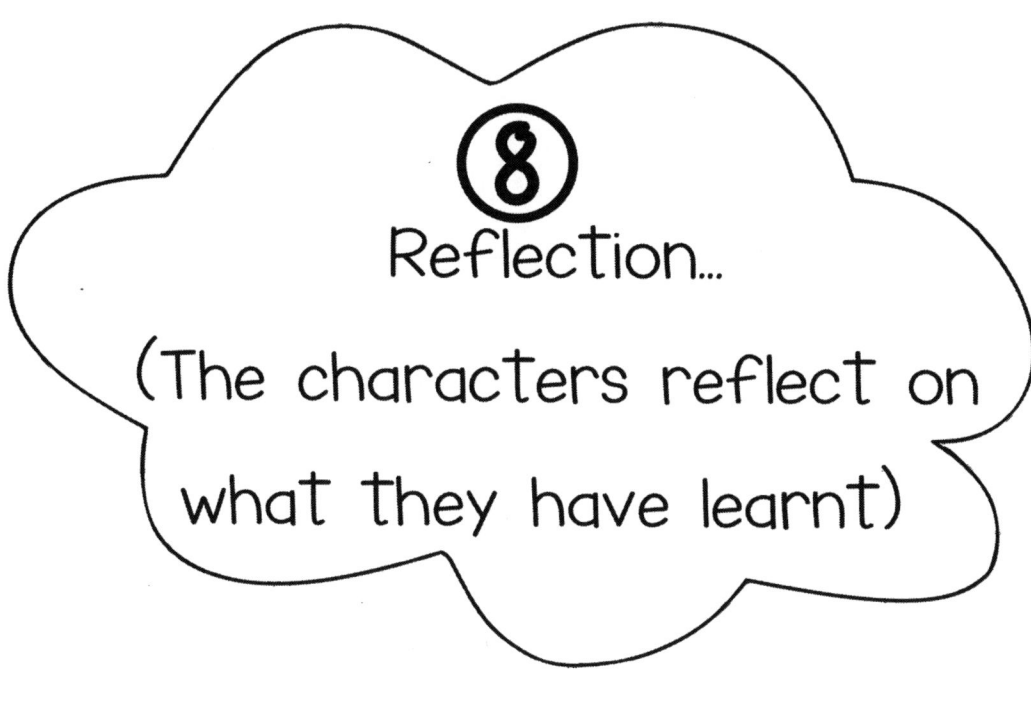

⑧ Reflection...
(The characters reflect on what they have learnt)

Top Tip! Tie up all the loose ends.

THE END

Story Two

Write a storyboard summary for your story

1. This is a story about...	2. Who lives in...
3. When...	4. So...
5. But...	6. However...
7. In the end...	8. Reflection

PLOT MAP

① This is a story about... (meet the characters)

Top Tip
Start your story with action.

Plot Map

② Who live in... (Show the characters in their world)

Top Tip
Include smells and sounds.

PLOT MAP

③ When... (Something happens to change things)

Top Tip
This should change everything.

PLOT MAP

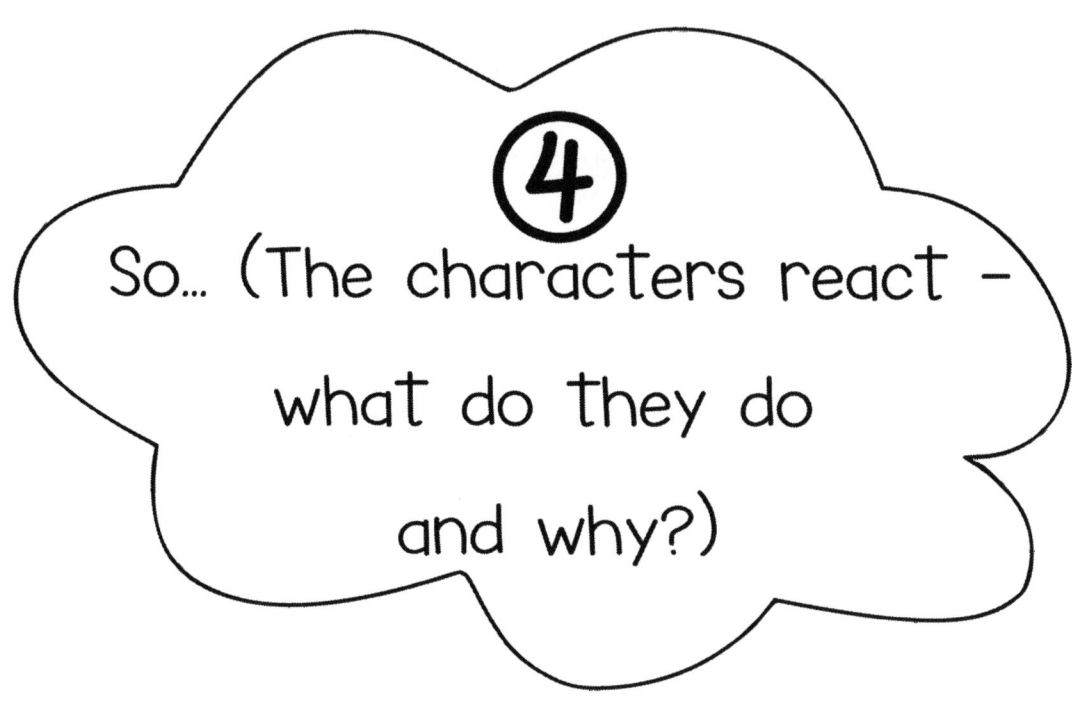

④ So... (The characters react – what do they do and why?)

Top Tip
Get them out of their comfort zone!

Plot Map

⑤ But...! (Something goes wrong)

Top Tip
All is hopeless...
or is it?

PLOT MAP

⑥ However...
(Your character tries to solve the problem)

Top Tip
Your character's special difference could help here.

Plot Map

⑦ In the end...(Do they succeed?)

Top Tip
You could include a final confrontation with your villain!

PLOT MAP

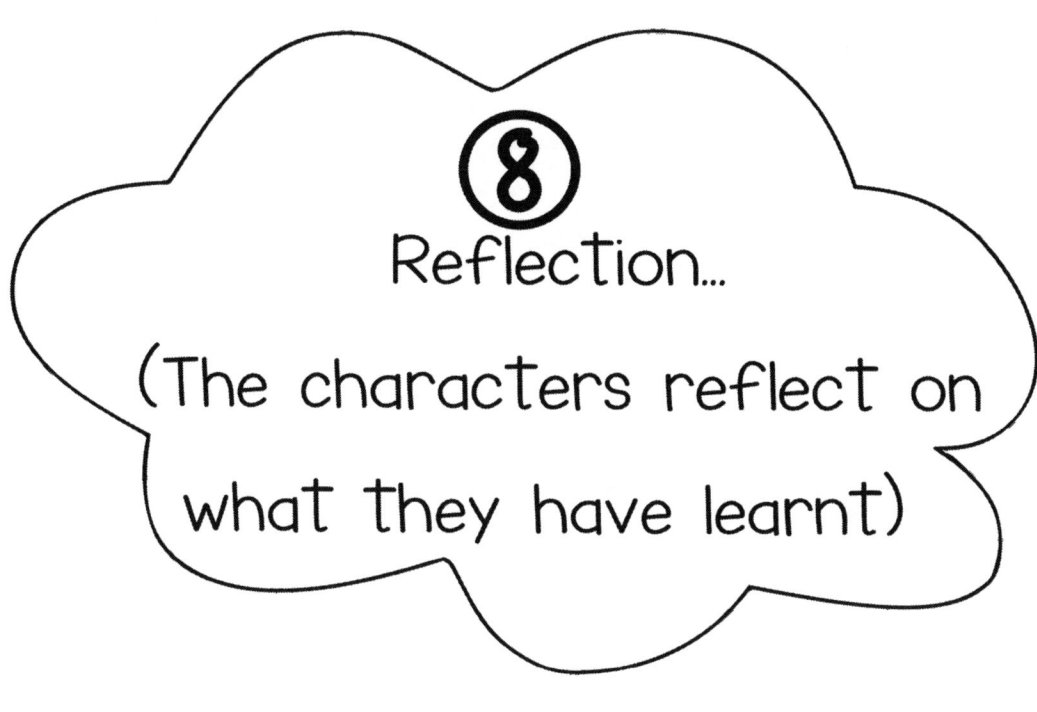

⑧ Reflection...

(The characters reflect on what they have learnt)

Top Tip! Tie up all the loose ends.

Story Three

Write a storyboard summary for your story

1. This is a story about…

2. Who lives in…

3. When…

4. So…

5. But…

6. However…

7. In the end…

8. Reflection

Plot Map

① This is a story about...
(meet the characters)

Top Tip
Start your story with action.

Plot Map

② Who live in... (Show the characters in their world)

Top Tip Include smells and sounds.

Plot Map

③ When... (Something happens to change things)

Top Tip
This should change everything.

PLOT MAP

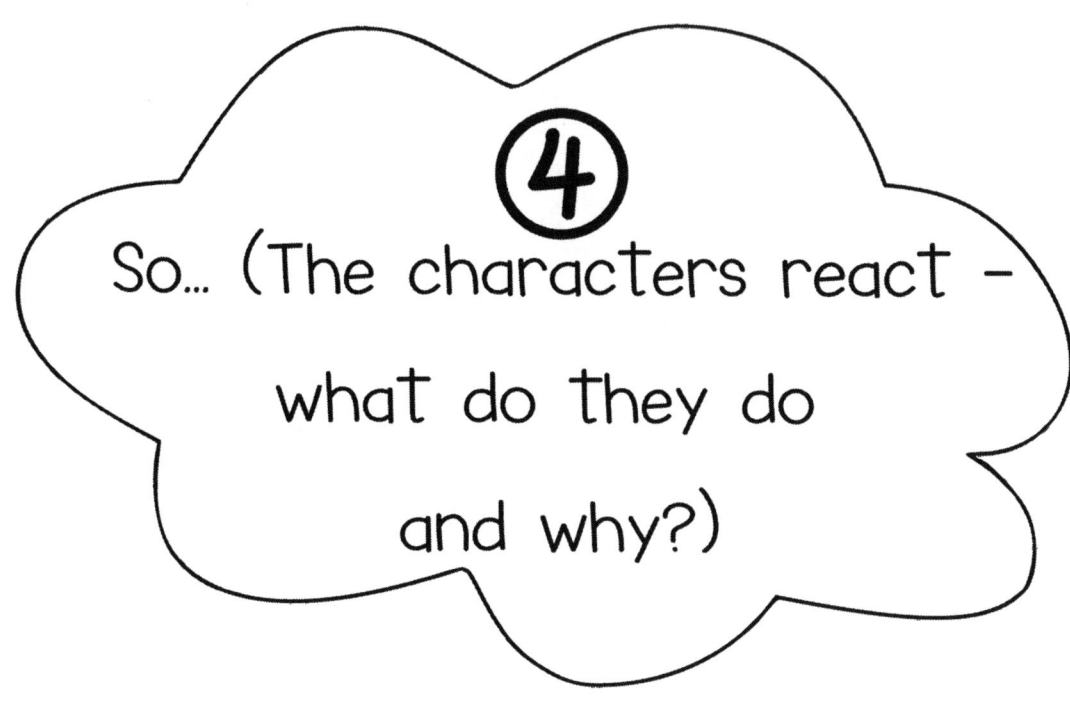

④ So... (The characters react – what do they do and why?)

Top Tip
Get them out of their comfort zone!

Plot Map

⑤ But...! (Something goes wrong)

Top Tip
All is hopeless...
or is it?

Plot Map

6 However...

(Your character tries to solve the problem)

Top Tip
Your character's special difference could help here.

Plot Map

⑦ In the end…(Do they succeed?)

Top Tip
You could include a final confrontation with your villain!

PLOT MAP

⑧ Reflection...

(The characters reflect on what they have learnt)

Top Tip! Tie up all the loose ends.

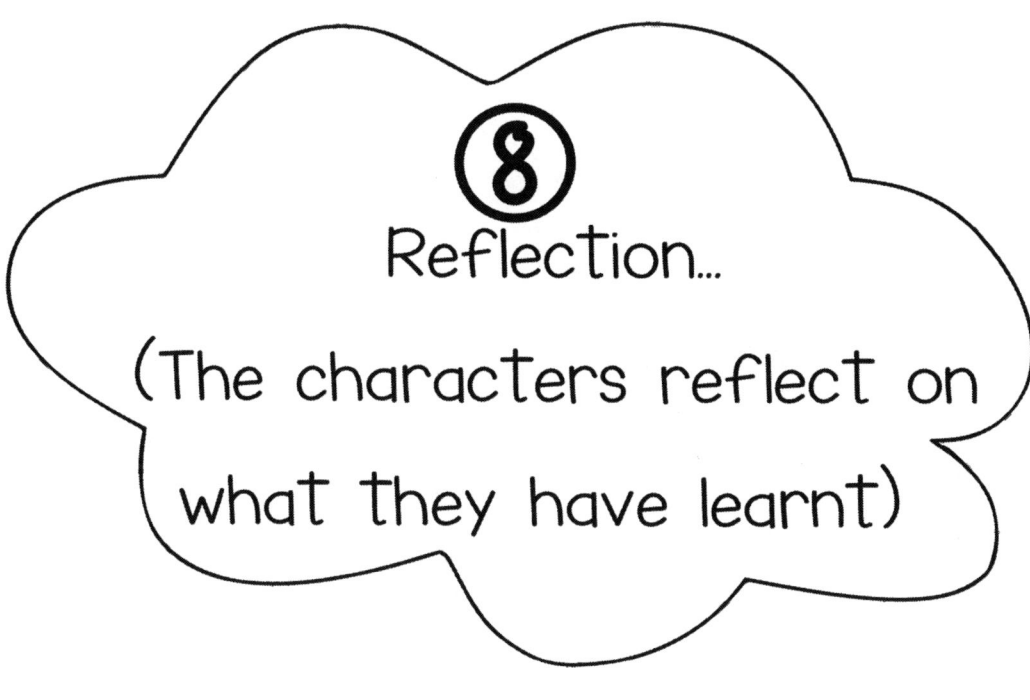

THE END

Look out for the other 'You Can Write a Story' Books

If you enjoyed writing your stories, please leave a review to help others find this book and write their stories too!

Made in the USA
Columbia, SC
24 September 2023